LLAUGH

How Laughter, Love, Abundance, Understanding, Gratitude & Hope helped me heal & opened my heart to living a fuller, more meaningful life.

Christopher Zurcher
and Rachel Heerema

To my niece and nephew

I was going to use the Neil Young quotation about the chrome heart here, from his song "Long May You Run" but it takes a lot to make that happen! (It's Google-able)

Here I was going to use the Rachel Naomi Remen quotation about the way we deal with loss and how it shapes our capacity to be present ....
https://onbeing.org/programs/rachel-naomi-remen-the-difference-between-fixing-and-healing-nov2018

Here I liked the quotation about laughter being the key to your heart from
the Crosby Stills and Nash song "Suite: Judy Blue Eyes."

CONTENTS

I wrote this book in large part, as many books are, as therapy and with the hope that others might benefit from my experience.

It's about coming close to dying at the age of 54 and how I dealt with that. This time (I have come close before) it was mostly as an adult.

When I came close before it was at a much younger age – 18 years – still very much a child. I was hit by a car while riding my bicycle across the country for disarmament. That was in the summer of 1982, just after graduating from high school.

I came close to dying again when I was about 23 years old – still very young. The car I was driving rear-ended the car in front of me while I was on my way from Tampa to Atlanta to see a Grateful Dead show at the Fox Theater. Despite my continued attempts after impact, we never made it to the show. We were severely bruised though. From head to toe.

Another time, I think this was the last one, I was sleeping in my second-floor bedroom when lightning struck an ungrounded radio antenna that belonged to the landlord next door. The fire marshall's report said that, because the ground wire was broken, the lightning went right into the attic (which was right above my kitchen) and started a fire. The firemen woke me up at 1:30 a.m. and said, "take one thing and get out of the building. There's a fire."

I grabbed my guitar and went out to stand in the pouring rain. After watching them drench the inside of the building (the rain was taking care of the outside) I drove to my office in New Haven and went to sleep on a piece of cardboard on the floor.

This book, though, is about another incident – going through emergency heart surgery in 2017; recovering from that; and the thoughts and feelings surrounding that. I thought those thoughts and feelings were important enough to write them down and I wanted to try and organize them in a way that came to me in a rare moment of clarity.

I want to thank my wife, Rachel Heerema, who was there at every step of the way during the surgery and recovery. She continues to be an anchor and an inspiration and she is co-author, since some of her words appear in these pages along with my own.

My family was also there and traveled from far away to be there when I was in intensive care. I asked my wife to filter friends' requests to come and see me, but I want to thank all of them for their prayers and positive vibes while I was in the hospital and while I was recovering at home. I want to thank Mary and Bob, Stirling, Neal, Howard, Joe, and everyone else who lent a hand in preparing the manuscript. While I'm sure it is far from perfect, it is much better than it would have been without the help and input of many people. And, I think, it is good enough. As I've told innumerable people, there are other writing projects that I want to get to, so I'm finishing it up and putting it out there. I apologize for any errors that make it more difficult to read had I gotten a real publisher and not done everything myself.

And I thank you the reader, for reading it, or for at least giving it a shot. Any links that appear in the printed matter or in the e-book version are for reference purposes only. I don't receive payment for those.

Sincerely,
Christopher Zurcher

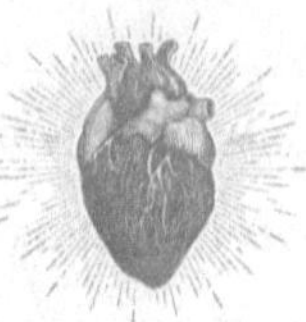

You don't usually survive a ruptured aorta. The operative note describes it as a "contained rupture of ascending aorta just distal to RCA (right coronary artery)." And a Bentall procedure with a bioprosthetic valve and 30mm graft. (There are lots of neat diagrams online if you Google this stuff!)

"You're a very lucky man, Mr. Zurcher," the surgeon said when he entered the examination room. I was there for my three-month post-op visit. It had been three months since he had repaired a contained ruptured aorta on the operating table and replaced my insufficient aortic valve.

"I am so thankful, and my wife sends her thanks, too, for saving my life. We are both so grateful," I said, emphasizing the "so" thankful, "so" grateful and explaining that I was overcome with emotion, the tears already welling up in my eyes.

"That's alright," he said.

"How is your wife, Rachel?" he said, remembering her name.

"She is doing really well," I said.

Shaking his head, he turned to sit down and said, "Poor woman."

We were on the other side of something that nearly took my life just three-and-a-half months into my marriage to the most beautiful, funniest, most fun, smartest person I have ever known.

Backstory

In November of 2010, a friend of ours introduced me to Rachel. I was working on a project called Pinwheels for Peace that would bring the city's elementary school students together in a community art and peace project on the green. Rachel knew the ins and outs of renting the green for events. She was the go-to person for a lot of things "community" in town.

We scheduled a meeting at a small I in downtown, Koffee on Audubon (www.koffeefamily.com), for January, which was two months away. It seemed like a long time to wait.

I Googled her and found out that she was the director of a local youth organization and had similar political views as I.

While visiting my parents that Christmas, I showed them a picture of Rachel on Facebook. My father said she looked very pretty. My mother said she had a nice smile.

When we met in January, I learned not only who to talk to about renting the green but that, like me, Rachel wasn't a coffee drinker. I learned that she was well connected, well-spoken, kind, shared similar values, and she was a beautiful human being and brilliant. I found that she was smarter than me, too, which means I liked her.

Rachel told me later that after the meeting, she walked away, thinking, "He likes me! He likes me!" Since I had just broken up with someone a couple of months before we first met, so I wasn't in a hurry to get involved with anyone at that time. Five months later, we went on our first real date.

Over the intervening five months, we saw each other several times at the local co-working space where I was working on my Connecticut environmental news blog with some community partners.

I asked Rachel for some help online with something having to do with Facebook, and she helped me fix whatever it was. I said that, in return, I owed her a beer. She said maybe next week. I said, "How about tomorrow?" She said, "Fine." The date took place Friday, May 27, 2011. We went to Mango's, which has since closed, just outside of New Haven in Branford. We had a beer and shared quite a few laughs. Rachel reinforced my impression that she is the funniest person I've ever met.

That was when she invited me to a gathering of a few of her friends for drinks at Kelly's downtown (also since closed) to celebrate her birthday the following Friday. I said in my typical non-committal way that I would try to make it. I was the last one to arrive and the last one to leave.

We continued dating. We spent an evening at TNT Seafood and Grill that shared a space with Rita's Ice Cream shop (also since closed. Am I dating myself here?). We started to get to know one another a little there and had some intense conversation about who we were and how we'd grown up. On another date, this time at Outback Steakhouse, after we'd both had a bad day, we ended up laughing so hard we drew the attention of neighboring tables and the wait staff. Part of the evening involved building tall, eventually tumbling, towers of drink coasters.

Not long after that, Rachel had a trip planned to Long Island with her parents. It was too early in the relationship for me to join her. After that, she went to California for a conference. By this time, I think we were officially "partners." Later that year, around summertime, she refused an offer from my family to join us on a Caribbean cruise on a very large cruise ship. In December, weeks before the trip, she changed her mind and went with us.

In August of the following year, Rachel sold her condo and moved into my apartment with me. I had a hard time convincing her that she could live with me rather than with her parents, but that October, Rachel bought a house and we moved in together. Before the end of that October, Hurricane Sandy visited the Eastern Coastline. We got a knock on the door on October 28, ordering us to evacuate the house ahead of Sandy's landfall. First, we booked a room in nearby Branford. But we soon decided to travel further inland to Hartford. We packed a cooler with enough sandwiches and snacks for a few days and took to the roads.

Four years later, in 2016, we were married.

Three months later, my GP said I had a heart

murmur. "Probably nothing to worry about, but something I want you to get checked out."

The echocardiogram indicated "aortic insufficiency," which the doctor (not a cardiologist) presented to me as "something to keep an eye on."

I learned later that the usual measurement of the aorta on these reports is 3.7cm. According to the echocardiogram itself, mine was 5.4cm. But at that time, I hadn't read the entire report and didn't think I would have to or would even understand anything on it. That was a mistake. From now on, I always look at the reports as soon as they are available to see if there's anything I can understand and if there's anything anyone has missed or that raises concerns in my mind. (Always read your reports as soon as you can, even if you're not sure you'll be able to understand them. Ask your doctor for help reading them if you have to!)

According to the medical malpractice conglomerate in town, the 5.4cm measurement should have been "an immediate cardiology consult." That wasn't the only breakdown in the system that I nearly paid for with my life.

Apparently, back pain can also be a sign of aortic insufficiency. Mine, according to an orthopedist, was because I was getting old. I told him in

December that I thought I'd hurt my back reading in bed while lying on my stomach. He sat back in his chair without so much as examining me and asked, "How old are you?" That was his answer. I was "getting older." Not a thought of possible heart trouble. Not a check of other symptoms or my medical history. Unfortunately, the echocardiogram came after this visit, after a referral to a back doctor and after a prescription for Flexeril. Well, guess what, Doc?

Better than the alternative

I visited my general practitioner a few months after the incident.

He came in partly astonished to see me and with a few things already on his mind to express.

"Guess what?" I said, "I don't have any ankle or foot swelling anymore."

I had asked him about my swollen ankles for a couple of years, not knowing any better. I know now that a good Google search of "dilated aortas" and measurements and such, that swelling in the feet and legs is an indicator of a dilated aorta and aortic insufficiency. That is just what my GP and a Yale cardiologist who read the echocardiogram results said I had, and it's what he told me was "something to keep an eye on."

Back to my GP.

"Doc, I like you," I said, but I wasn't feeling calm on the inside. "I'm not suggesting that you did anything wrong. You noticed the murmur. You scheduled the echocardiogram. You're a good doctor. It was good we had the echo on file."

I paused before continuing, weighing my words.

"You just almost weren't good enough for me. I was almost gone for good. You almost weren't good enough."

I still don't know if that was his fault or the fault of the cardiologist who read the results of the echocardiogram, or if it's anyone's fault, or maybe everyone's.

If I'd have seen a cardiologist after the holidays, then maybe they would have scheduled an echo from inside my throat before I'd had the emergency. Maybe they would have seen the dissected aorta, rather than waiting until it nearly knocked me out while driving home on I-95 the night of Jan. 3, 2017. Maybe it wasn't there at that time. I just don't know. What I do know is: according to a top medical malpractice lawyer, an aortic root measurement of 5.4 cm, like my echo showed I had, was enough for "an immediate surgical consult."

I don't know what any of the answers are. They're all 'maybe this' and 'maybe that.' I just know that my doctor was observant enough to notice the murmur. And that was a good thing and something for which I'm grateful. It was good to have the echocardiogram on hand when I was in the Emergency Room. I just wish that had been enough of a warning a week before to have avoided the Emergency Room.

"Well, you survived," he said. "And how are you doing?"

"Getting older, I guess," I said.

"Well, it's better than the alternative."

The Timeline: Mailing packages for the holidays and buying stamps

Around the same time that we got married, my then 83-year-old father repeated his suggestion to my three siblings and me that we see cardiologists because he has A-fib, and he has a pacemaker, and his father had a bad valve replaced, and these things can be genetic. "Just as a precaution and just to be safe," he said.

Since I had a physical coming up in December, I waited until the physical to get a recommendation for a cardiologist from my GP, if I needed one.

I had been seeing my GP for some years and had had a couple dozen physical exams with him and knew the procedure. But when he held the stethoscope on my chest and listened longer than he usually did, I had an inkling that something was up.

"I hear a murmur," he said. "It's nothing to be alarmed about … at this point," he said, "but I think we should schedule an echocardiogram." He pressed some keys on his laptop and scheduled an appointment for me at Yale New Haven Hospital at 3:30 p.m. the Friday before Christmas.

Googling "heart murmur," one finds the Mayo Clinic description as such: "A person with an innocent murmur has a normal heart … An abnormal heart murmur is more serious … In adults, abnormal murmurs are most often due to acquired heart valve problems."

The technician doing the exam isn't allowed to interpret what they see on the screen. They're just there to take the pictures and recordings of your heartbeat and try to measure the distances between things (like the walls of the aorta in different places) and measure the volume of ventricles and the strength of the heart in general.

I tried, to no avail, to get some sort of information. It was 4 p.m. the Friday before Christmas, and all the tech would tell me is that the cardiologist was going over the results. I thought that was pretty conscientious of them and looked forward to learning more about my heart and the source of the murmur once they figured it out.

I had watered the Christmas tree that morning, and Rachel was making chili. I had mailed Christmas presents to my family. While December was a time when we talked a lot about going out and doing things in the community, we stayed home that night. We enjoyed a fire in the fireplace with a glass of wine and some ciabatta bread and oil and vinegar and olives – something Bistro Mediterranean in East Haven does for its customers while they wait for their appetizers or meal.

The following week I received a voice mail message from my GP who said I had an insufficient aorta and that it was something to keep an eye on. It was a couple of days past Christmas, and nothing-to-worry-about was enough of a gift for me.

Along with this information, I received a two-

and-a-half-page document via Yale's online patient communication portal called MyChart, explaining that I had a mild concentric ventricular hypertrophy and a dilated aorta measuring 5.4cm in the sinuses of Valsalva, whatever that means. (I didn't think I'd understand much of the report, and I trusted the doctors at Yale to interpret it for me. It wasn't until later that I looked at it more closely and discovered that it also said the high end of the average measurement was 3.7cm.)

If I had read it when I received it, then I think I would have been able to convince my doctor to schedule some more exams, particularly a CT Scan.

So, for the time being, I had something called "aortic insufficiency," which is something to keep an eye on. Okay. On with my life.

Happy New Year

In mid-December, Rachel was reviewing $400-$500/month insurance options (now even more since then), and we were texting back and forth about what we were planning to have for dinner. Rachel was meeting her friends at the Shubert Theater for a performance by Pink Martini. Her friend, who wore stiletto heels, had the opportunity, along with many others, to dance with the band (her favorite) on stage. Unfortunately, thanks to those stiletto heels and the dancing, Rachel's friend ended up in the Emergency Room from breaking her ankle in several places that night.

Around that time, I saw the orthopedist about my back pain at a clinic they have after working hours. Rachel texted me whether I told him how helpful massage had been. I had, but he told me I was "getting old" and gave me a prescription for a muscle relaxant anyway and referred me to a spine doctor.

Rachel texted WTF?

I responded with "What?"

She responded with "I hate allopathic medicine."

On Dec. 20, Rachel texted, asking how my doctor's appointment went with my GP. I said he heard a murmur and was scheduling an echocardiogram. A reminder to check the water in the Christmas tree was another one of my texts to Rachel.

"Come home, my love. Warmth awaits you."

These are the kinds of texts I sometimes get from my wife, Rachel, during the coldest days of winter.

"Our front steps are now Christmas swag-tastic," is another one.

On Dec. 28, I texted Rachel in response to one of

her texts that, yes, I would like to have dinner with her along with my mother-in-law, and my niece and nephew. Also, "I don't have anything seriously wrong with my heart," I continued. "Just a weak valve, I think. That's what the doctor heard. That's why I saw red and blue on the monitor at the same time (when I was getting my echocardiogram the week before). Aortic insufficiency."

"Ohh, hmmm, we'll have to do some internet research on that," she wrote back.

"I start various low to medium exercises at least 15 minutes two or three times a day. No more excuses," I wrote back. "Even if it's dancing in the kitchen. I have to do more. I read that being sedentary makes it worse."

"I love you," she wrote back. "You are going to be healthy and vigorous and happy with me for a long time <3<3<3<3<3<3<3<3." (those are texted hearts).

After a rather sleepy, cozy New Years, I started back at work.

Jan 1.

The hawks seemed to be everywhere. It seemed like everywhere I drove, a redtail or some other kind of hawk would pass over my car, or over the road in front of me. I can tell hawks from seagulls and osprey and crows and turkey vultures. So I'm not just saying "hawks" for hawks' sake. If you believe in spirit animals, it was like Mother Nature was trying to tell me something. I'm not sure how much I believe in spirit animals, but I don't NOT believe in them, put it that way.

According to Colleen McCann on Goop.com (https://goop.com/style/trends/guide-spirit-animals), some believe that we travel with a cadre of spiritual guides, including animals. They can be harnessed, so to speak, through meditation or in totem form.

I don't know where I was going on Jan 1, 2017, but I texted Rachel: "I want to know what the hawk is trying to tell me." This after weeks of seeing hawks overhead and many times flying over my car.

"Ask the spirit of the hawk to tell you," she wrote.

"Together, we can make it big somehow," she wrote on Jan 2. "I've been amazed at how wonderful my life has become since you came along."

Tuesday, Jan. 3, was cold, rainy and gloomy. That morning we were talking about a way to stop Donald Trump. We laughed. It was a joke, in more ways than one.

"We should find a reason to sue him and stop his inauguration," I said.

It was a cold, gray drive to work. It hadn't started raining yet, but it was a typically gray, New Haven day. I had a few clients who were in nursing homes and who I was trying to find affordable, accessible housing they could move into. One, let's call him Herb, was due to move out the following day. There were some calls that needed to be made, and emails sent to confirm the nursing home knew he was scheduled to leave and to confirm the leasing office knew he was scheduled to move in. Coordinating housing for this particular state program is a job in which no stone can be left unturned, and no calls or emails can be left unsent. The principle I learned a long time ago of CYA (Cover Your Ass) is an essential rule to live by. People who are desperate to leave where they are, depend on things going smoothly, which rarely happens in any bureaucracy, and, I think I can honestly say, never happens in the one I work for.

I skipped lunch. I had chocolate and drank water. I stopped in the bathroom before leaving around 5:45 p.m. for the half-hour drive home. Being a little late, I was in a bit of a hurry to get out of the office.

Everything came out fine, as they say. Flush. Wash. Turn out the lights. Lock the door.

Texting about dinner that day and what we had in stock in our refrigerator, Rachel wrote: "It's pouring out. Not sure if I'll be able to drag myself to the grocery store for bread."

"We have bread," I said.

"We have crappy bread, not garlic bread worthy. Do you think Krausczer's has Apicella's?"

"Prolly not," I wrote back. "I'll see."

"<3<3<3" (hearts again).

It was dark, and the rain was coming down in buckets.

Shortly after getting on the highway, I heard one of the NPR broadcasters say that various parties were asking Trump to reveal his business interests and conflicts of interest before his inauguration.

Really not looking forward to our newly elected president's inauguration, I did a fist pump, hitting the steering wheel of my 2004 Ford Focus I was driving, grunting almost under my voice "fuck Trump, fuck Trump, fuck Trump" with each fist pump.

That's when it hit me.

A second later, I could hardly breathe.

Something was terribly wrong. I felt like I had a cue ball in the center of my chest.

My anxiety level went through the roof in zero seconds flat.

Thank you, Donald. And you are welcome. You are more powerful than you know. (This I say tongue-in-cheek.)

The Event

Not being able to breathe gives one a strong sense that something is going terribly awry somewhere.

"Do I need to stop what I'm doing? Take some deep breaths?

"I CAN'T! I can't take deep breaths. It feels like if I take deep breaths, I'm going to puncture a lung, and then I'll really be in trouble. It's also near my heart. Whatever is happening feels dangerously close to my heart. It's in my chest. My heart is in my chest. I don't know what's going on."

It had been a week after the aortic insufficiency diagnosis. I was on I-95 driving in the dark in early January in the pouring rain. I called Rachel in a panic.

I always wondered what would happen if I had a

mild heart attack while I was driving. Was this it? Should I pull over? Would I soon be unconscious and endangering the lives of other drivers. I'd written a short story about something like this. I didn't want this to end the way that did.

I was lucky in more ways than I can count. One way is that I had only experienced shortness of breath while driving. Googling the condition that I suffered (dissected aorta), the results reveal symptoms of "fainting, stroke, and paralysis" – not good symptoms if you're driving on a major interstate and wishing to live longer (or choose what exit you're going to take instead of having your exit forced on you).

Another way I was lucky is that my incredibly loving wife, Rachel, answered the phone.

"What do I do? I don't know what to do," I said.

"What's happening?" she asked.

"I love you. I can't breathe normally. I'm on my way home. I just left Clinton. I'm on I-95. I don't know what to do. Oh, my God. I love you so much. I don't know what's happening. I'm sorry." I was crying, but I was trying as hard as I could to not lose complete control. I usually like to be in control.

"What's happening? Slow down and tell me what's happening," she said.

"I can't breathe normally, only about half of what I could a minute ago. I love you. I don't know what to do. Oh, my God. I love you."

At this point, and this was early on in the process, I was really afraid I was very close to dying. And I had been close, as we found out later.

Rachel later admitted that she thought it might have been too much Stromboli at lunch that was causing me distress.

"Pull over," she said. "Hang up with me and call 911."

Then, like a vision from Heaven, the I-95 Madison South Bound Service Plaza appeared.

"Oh, my God. There's the rest area. I'm pulling over. I'll call 911. I love you." I'd never in my 53 ½ years been happier to see a rest area.

"Yes. Pull over. Stay calm. Call an ambulance. Call me when you're in the ambulance. Don't forget to call me and tell me what's happening."

I pulled into the rest stop. I looked for a recognizable spot. The handicapped spots were empty in front of the Dunkin' Donuts. I took the handicapped tag that I seldom used out of my glove compartment and hung it on the mirror and pulled in. My heart felt tight. Like I had a ball the size of my fist in the center of my chest. I could only breathe short breaths.

I waited and told the 911 operator how I had just gotten married in September and how much I loved my wife and how well we got along. I was crying. I was scared.

I wanted to tell everyone I knew I loved them. I wanted more than anything to live. I pleaded with God to let me live. To have this be a minor incident. The operator tried to assure me that everything was going to be okay.

I hoped I wouldn't get towed if I left my car where I was parked. I looked around for a sign that might say, "No overnight parking." That was the least of my worries.

At 6:05 p.m., Rachel texted me, "What's happening?!" I was probably on the phone with the 911 operator at the time. It wasn't much later that she called my phone and the EMT in the back of the ambulance, who was feeding me baby aspirin and nitroglycerin, answered. I had forgotten to call her. Rachel was at the ER waiting when we arrived.

Another way I was lucky was that I had skipped lunch. As I would explain to dozens of people before being wheeled into surgery a couple of hours later, I had skipped lunch that day, which was fortunate because the anesthesiologist depends in part on the patient having an empty stomach. All I had eaten that day was a bit of chocolate. By the time I went into surgery, it had been about 6 hours before I had even had chocolate and probably 12 hours or more since breakfast.

Rachel, who had arrived at the Yale New Haven Hospital Emergency Room before the ambulance arrived, watched them gingerly transfer me from the ambulance stretcher to a hospital gurney directing me not to move a muscle.

About 12 hours later, after about 6 hours of emergency open-heart surgery, Rachel learned that I had suffered from a dissected aorta and that, while I was on the operating table, that dissection had turned into a ruptured aorta. A dissected aorta is bad enough. Luckily for me, the rupture was found while I was on the operating table – another stroke of luck: right place, right time.

Generally, one does not survive a ruptured aorta. (According to Wikipedia: "Mortality from aortic rupture is up to 90%. 65-75% of patients die before they arrive at the hospital, and up to 90% die before they reach the operating room." https://en.wikipedia.org/wiki/Aortic_rupture.) Luckily for me, I was in the operating room and already undergoing open-heart surgery. They also replaced with a new valve what had been described in the December echocardiogram report as "aortic insufficiency."

The experience of the emergency surgery and subsequent recovery that Rachel and I shared brought us closer than we ever imagined we could be or would be, especially after three months of marriage. That is what inspired this book, which is more of a set of meditations on the ingredients of my recovery and, perhaps, recovery in general – Laughter, Love, Abundance, Understanding, Gratitude, and Hope – LLAUGH.

I am reminded of the pre-marital counseling sessions in Pastor Shelly's office months before: "What are you willing to do for one another? When worse comes to worst, what are you willing to do?" Pastor Shelly crossed her arms, tilted her head and looked at us. Then me.

"Chris? What are you willing to do?"

Me first?

I said that I thought I would be willing to do anything. Having been in intensive care before (for a month in 1982) and having had a visiting nurse visit regularly for various reasons, I had a pretty good idea of what "anything" meant.

Well, this aortic experience put us to the test, and

many of the results are in this book for others to hopefully enjoy or benefit from, or both.

Now What?

You may not be able to imagine being faced with emergency surgery that you may or may not survive, and you may not be able to imagine how you might feel and what you might think if you ever have to face that, but your life really does flash before your eyes. Maybe you have experienced that. Maybe you have been on the stretcher and had someone bending over you saying, "You're going to be fine. I'm the anesthesiologist. I'm the doctor's assistant. I'll be doing this. I'll be doing that. Here's a warm blanket to make you feel more comfortable. Blah blah blah blah...."

People you love; things you have done and things you have not done; things that are incomplete; papers on your desk; things you have written down to do something about; recordings you have made; people you have met; and wanted to meet; things you have wanted to do; your siblings, long lost or not; your parents – dead or alive. If you don't fear death, it seems to me that you better have your affairs in order. I didn't. And one of the things I kept thinking about was, "God, I hope she doesn't get stuck with having to clean up all the crap in my office!" And also, most of all, I just don't feel I've really done what I think I've been put on this earth to do... yet. Some of these are things you think about when you wake up and realize what could have been or what might not have been.

When I realized that I had faced the possibility that I might not have made it out on the same side I went in on, it kicked me in the ass – big time – and lit a fire under me to get up and do the things I've wanted to do with my life. Writing this book is the first thing I wanted to do, and I hope you get something out of it.

For Rachel, the writing is the confirmation that I'm alive and that we are still here – "We made it to the other side: Down the rabbit hole and back out again."

As Rob Brezney writes: "We may believe that all of creation is conspiring to shower us with blessings. And that life is crazily in love with us – brazenly and innocently in love with us. And that the universe always gives us exactly what we need, exactly when we need it. And that the winds and the tides are on our side, forever and ever, amen. And that the fire and the rain are scheming to steal our pain. And that the sun and the moon and the stars remember our real names and our ancestors pray for us while we're dreaming. And that we have guardians we can't even imagine – spirit animals, brothers and sisters, or nieces and nephews – who want us to blossom. And that thanks to them from whom the blissful blessings flow, we are waking up.

But what if we don't believe that? What DO we believe? Do we believe that everything happens for a reason? Did I almost die on my way home from work for a reason? Would my death have been for a reason? If a loved one dies today, is it for a reason? Is there some greater lesson to be learned? To be taught?

This early passage from Brezny's beautiful book "Pronoia" (subtitled "The Antidote for Paranoia") is a wonderful world view to wake up to, as he puts it. That we are surrounded, even if we can't see them, by teachers and provocateurs, helpers and saviors, brothers and sisters who want us to blossom. It, to me, is reassuring, to say the least … if we can believe it. That our ancestors are praying for us, and there are things scheming to steal our "impossible pain." And, that the universe always gives us what we need when we need it.

I've been told that, since my open heart surgery,

my heart chakra is more open than it ever was. Some of the questions I wonder about now include:

Do I have more love for others and life in general now than I did before?

- Am I more compassionate?
- Do I accept myself more?
- Am I more inclined to give?
- Do I have a better sense of well-being and balance?
- Are my physical and spiritual planes more integrated?
- Am I more selfless?
- Do I have more control over my senses and emotions?
- Do I have a balance of the female and male energies within myself? And,
- Is there more harmony in my relationships?

So, while I'm no expert on chakras or opening them or doing anything else with them, through the opening of this fourth chakra (the middle chakra among seven that exist), the one that I've been told is an essential part of some spiritual traditions, it becomes "the mediator for divine love and access to non-dual states where there is only love, where the one who loves and the object of love, the lover and the beloved are one." (www.chakras.info)

Now, I doubt that I will begin to see love in anything and everything, but I do feel a bit more at peace than before my surgery. While I may interact with others in a graceful manner, don't expect me to trust anyone simply based on my having an open heart chakra.

Well, so much for the opening of the heart chakra, you might say.

Read on.…

Leo Babauta, of www.zenhabits.com, writes that our lives are spent anticipating more important moments when we'll be happy. But, when those moments don't come, we're no less happy than we were a moment ago and we already begin planning for the next trip, the next project, next get together with friends or family, the next pizza.

Then, he asks, "What if that wonderful moment we've been waiting for is this one, right now?"

I believe that NOW IS the next big moment. NOW is the only moment. NOW is all we know that we have. We're hopefully not waiting to die, but starting new every day.

If your wife or other loved one is downstairs or

in the other room, go kiss her, or him. Go tell them you love them. This is your legacy. This very moment is your legacy. It is for what you do now that you'll be remembered. Not what you're planning to do in two weeks. Because, as I found out, you might not be here in two weeks and, if this is the case, then what moment could possibly be more important than right now?

Life is just a series of Nows. Now. Now. Now. Now. Now. (Sorry, but that's it.)

We must learn to see what is in front of us and find ways to be grateful for this moment, for this one is the most brilliant that may ever be.

When I turned toward my pain – toward the realization that I wanted to sleep in the master bedroom again, for example, even if it meant crawling up the stairs to do so; I wanted to sleep with my wife again; I wanted those intimate moments to begin again; I wanted to take out the garbage so my wife didn't have to; I wanted to go to the grocery store myself; I wanted to shovel the snow from the sidewalk and the stairs, (Really I did!). And I wanted to stand in the shower, not sit on the plastic shower chair with the holes in it that leave marks on your butt flesh; I wanted to eat my own selection of foods and not take some chemicals that would ease my toileting while destroying my intestinal lining. When I was present with my pain and was kind towards it and accepted what I was going through and where I was in that process, that's when this most important moment of my life came to me. Yes, it was a flash. But it was not cliché.

Now, it's three years later as I write this, most of that pain is gone. Still, I must turn toward other things, like the question of what sort of legacy I'm creating. I might spend tens or hundreds and thousands of hours on the internet. How to leave a legacy? Spend your best hours working on what you are most passionate about, and in that which you most passionately believe.

What's going on? What is recovery? What is life? Of what does it consist?

The answer came to me in the mnemonic LLAUGH, which spells out the words *Laughter, Love, Abundance, Understanding, Gratitude,* and *Hope.*

I turned to Rachel. "I just had an idea," I said. This may have been through tears that were streaming down my face. I can't count the number of times just thinking of what happened to me, and the feelings that Rachel endured, and the loss she came so close to having to endure, brought tears to my eyes. In fact, it still happens to both of us. We still look at each other, and we know. We'll say, "I'm glad I'm alive." Or "I'm glad you're alive."

I told her about the LLAUGH idea, and she liked it.

I didn't feel I had a path for learning. I wasn't seeing a psychologist about my crying jags. About my deep emotionality about what I had been through. I didn't yet know the benefits of prescription CBD oil. I felt I was on solid ground, but I wasn't completely comfortable with everything that was in my mind about the event. I wasn't at peace. But, as many Zen Buddhists would agree, there is a way to be open to the ever-changing nature of life AND to be at peace with whatever life throws at you.

Rachel was in my life more than ever before. Three months married. Five plus years of being together.

Check out the lyrics of Bruce Cockburn's "Listen for the Laugh," from his Dart to the Heart album (https://youtu.be/uCIw2T5awiY).

I have a new understanding of the meaning of the word *Laughter.*

I have a new understanding of the meaning of the word *Abundance.*

I have a new understanding of the meaning of the word *Understanding*.

I have a new understanding of the meaning of the word *Gratitude*.

I have a new understanding of the meaning of the word *Hope*.

Most of all, I have a new understanding of the meaning of the word *Love*.

I hope that in these pages, if nothing else, I can convey that to you and every other reader out there.

LAUGHTER

"Tears, idle tears, I know not what they mean." ~ Alfred Lord Tennyson.

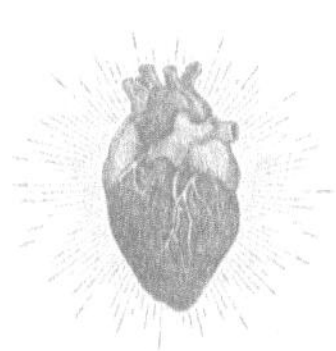

"Now, there's proof: Laughter really is the best medicine." That's the headline in The Telegraph (UK) article from Feb. 5, 2017. Subtitled like this: "Laughter is increasingly being used to cope with mental and physical ailments, from depression to chronic pain."

We don't have to define laughter. We all know

what laughter is. We all know the humor that suits our sensibilities and makes us smile and laugh. Some of us like the comedy of Lewis Black. Some of us don't. Some of us like George Carlin, some of us don't. But these things we know.

Didn't Norman Cousins not only write about it but live it?

Cousins, who was an Adjunct Professor of Medical Humanities for the School of Medicine at the University of California, Los Angeles, researched the biochemistry of human emotions. He believed they were the key to human beings' success in fighting illness, which he maintained as he battled a sudden-onset case of an unidentified, crippling illness tentatively diagnosed as ankylosing spondylitis.

This is the case for which he prescribed for himself massive intravenous doses of vitamin C. His recovery, he maintained, was accelerated by self-induced bouts of laughter brought on by a steady stream of videos of comic films like Laurel and Hardy. Some doubt the diagnosis of ankylosing spondylitis, and some have suggested that Cousins may actually have suffered from some type of reactive arthritis. His struggle with that illness is detailed in the book and movie "Anatomy of an Illness."

Later in life, he and his wife Ellen helped fight his heart disease, again with exercise, a daily regimen of vitamins, and with the good nutrition provided by Ellen's organic garden.

Cousins wrote a collection of best-selling non-fiction books on illness and healing, as well as a 1980 autobiographical memoir, "Human Options: An Autobiographical Notebook."

When Cousins was told that he had little chance of surviving, he developed his own recovery program. A long-time optimist who was known for his kindness to others, and for his robust love of life itself, Cousins wrote: "I made the joyous discovery that ten minutes of genuine belly laughter had an anesthetic effect and would give me at least two hours of pain-free sleep."

"When the pain-killing effect of the laughter wore off, [Ellen and I] would switch on the motion picture projector again and not infrequently, it would lead to another pain-free interval."

Laughing has been shown to release endorphins and reduce the stress hormones cortisol and epinephrine.

A study (http://umm.edu/news-and-events/news-releases/2005/school-of-medicine-study-shows-laughter-helps-blood-vessels-function-

<u>better</u>) found that it improves our circulation by dilating the inner lining of our blood vessels, boosting our immune system – up to 40 percent!

Some scientists say that prolonged laughter can lower blood pressure and improve our mental capacity.

When I asked my doctor (yes, the same one) whether my herniated belly button would have to be fixed, he just asked, "Is it painful?"

"No," I said.

"There could be worse things. Be happy she makes you laugh that much," he advised. Now I know it is the laugh of love.

According to Patch Adams (<u>https://en.wikipedia.org/wiki/Patch_Adams</u>), "Laughter boosts the immune system and helps the body fight off disease, cancer cells as well as viral, bacterial and other infections. Being happy is the best cure of all diseases!" Hunter Doherty "Patch" Adams is an American physician, comedian, social activist, clown, and author. He founded the Gesundheit! Institute in 1971 and writes that he is in the 49th year of building a "radical free" hospital in West Virginia! Every year he organizes volunteers from around the world to travel to various countries where they dress as clowns to bring humor to orphans, patients, and other people. Adams, in collaboration with the institute, promotes an alternative health care model not funded by insurance policies. The late Robin Williams played him in the movie named after Patch Adams.

But laughing isn't actually where the idea for this book arose. It came more from crying. But those tears were mostly tears of gratitude – gratitude for life following emergency heart surgery.

When I saw my first visitors at home a couple of weeks after the surgery – a friend from work and my boss, I said, "If I had died driving home from work, I never would have forgiven myself." (It's not about making a living. It's about living.)

While the language is a bit convoluted, it was not exactly a joke. If I had died driving home and could have looked back from the afterlife, I would have regretted having died while driving home from work, as opposed to flying home from a month in Hawaii, or the Grand Canyon, or Italy, or Switzerland.

The problem is that most of us have to work doing something, and if that something is not what we most love to do, then perhaps we can change our job or career.

But how do we know this? We don't. We don't

know where our minds go, where our thoughts go, where our feelings go, or where our souls go once our hearts stop beating, once we stop breathing, once we stop sustaining the living cells within our bodies. Once we die and are dead.

What do we do about what we've wanted to achieve in life?

What if we haven't yet achieved it?

What if our manuscript is sitting half-written on our desk at home, or, worse, on our password-protected laptop in our briefcase?

What if we're younger still and haven't yet gotten our dream job?

What if we haven't seen the Galapagos Islands? The Black Hills? The Northern Lights?

What if we haven't told our friends and loved ones we love them lately, or enough?

What's stopping us? Some people say life happens, as if life gets in the way. But that's no excuse.

"... Don't ask yourself if life is something that keeps you from living,

And try not to think that life is something that gets in the way."

~ from "Taking it for Granted" cjzurcher

What if we find ourselves on a stretcher being wheeled into surgery, kissing our wife of three months goodbye, telling her not to worry, and only being able to think of smiling in case this was the last time she was going to see us?

I couldn't even think of any profound quotations or things to say. I mostly didn't want to cry or make her worry any more than she already was. I didn't want to be morbid. Talk about the elephant in the room. There were 1,000 elephants in that Emergency Room that night, and they were all sitting on my chest!

"Smile, don't cry, just in case," I told myself.

That's exactly where I was on Jan. 3, 2017 – smiling as I was wheeled into surgery with a bit of worry. No. Honestly, I was terrified. And not just a bit of terror. Terror that I would lose my wife, and, worse, that she may lose me. That she would have to get a roommate to help pay the mortgage.

That she may have to try to meet someone else to marry and take care of her.

That she may give up hope of ever meeting someone and falling in love.

That she might feel cursed because her husband died of a ruptured aorta three months after their beautiful wedding in front of their family and friends that she did so much to make happen.

That I may never see her again. Make love with her again. Laugh with her again. See her laughing eyes. Hear her beautiful voice sing the Doxology with which the Church of the Redeemer (also closed) where we were married always began their service. (While we don't always make it to church Sunday morning, Rachel's faith is as strong as ever. She sang the Doxology as she drove back and forth to the hospital every day for a week to be by my side.)

I was smiling, but I was terrified that I might never cry with her again. Hold her in my arms again. Enjoy a vacation with her again, like I had just six months before for two blissful weeks in Italy and Switzerland.

That I might never feel the depth of her love and wisdom and spirit again.

Worried. About. Losing. Everything. And. Praying. I. Would. Not.

As they wheeled me down the hall to the operating room, I didn't know what more I could say any more than "I love you." I couldn't think of anything more to do than to smile. I prayed that not only would my life be spared but that all would be forgiven, all my transgressions, whatever troubles I'd caused anyone. I prayed for peace for myself and the world whatever happened. Not to be morbid, but I prayed for a peaceful afterlife, if that's where I was headed. I prayed that the next life, if there was one, would be less challenging than this one has been.

I learned that the most hopeless feeling is to approach the operating room on a stretcher not knowing the odds but being repeatedly reassured that I would be okay. I'm sure they tell that to everyone.

This is where I was while being rolled on a stretcher down the hall closely followed by Rachel so she could kiss me one ~~last~~ more time (not one last time, one more time) before the doors swung open and the warm blanket descended on my body that was quickly being undressed.

What words are there in that moment? The only words I knew to say, or think at that moment and not get upset, were "I Love You."

After casually awaiting the diagnosis, the surgeon arrived at the hospital and everything became rushed and urgent.

You just get on the plane. You trust the pilot to take off and land safely. You trust the plane is in good shape. You trust in whatever it is that you have faith in.

These are some of the many questions I faced, or tried to answer, or wrap my head around, or however you want to put it. These are the questions that start the tears. They still do, and I suspect they always will.

Ad Vingerhoets (professor of social and behavioral sciences at Tilburg University) lists states of helplessness and loss, personal conflict, anger, rejection, feelings of inadequacy, self-pity, joy, and the emotions produced just by the music in films (aeon magazine) as tear-producing causes. For Vingerhoets, "tears can be produced either by emotional isolation, or by an emotional encounter with another, either by loss and sorrow, or by success and joy."

So we have love. And we love to laugh. We have mostly everything we need. We don't argue or fight, so we have understanding. We're grateful. And we have faith and its close cousin, hope.

These are the questions that were brought to mind as I turned to my beautiful wife of now nearly five months to tell her of the LLAUGH meditation. "Laughter, Love, Abundance, Understanding, Gratitude, and Hope."

Laughter, because it's good for us.

Love, because, as the Beatles sang: "All we need is love."

Abundance, because regardless of how I felt three weeks after open-heart surgery, we had a roof over our heads; a beautiful house; a stocked refrigerator; a car to get to the store to restock it when needed; a snowblower; a neighbor with a plow who helped when it was needed; family that is praying for us and visiting us when we're ill; and more and more and more. Abundance. We were and are still blessed with so much – so many friends. Loving family. You can't say more about it other than it's a blessing. That's about the highest praise and recognition.

Understanding because we need to understand ourselves and how others relate to us in the good times and the bad.

Gratitude because it all comes down to gratitude. Being grateful for what you have and not begrudging what you don't will get you through to tomorrow and will make you thankful at the end of every day.

Hope. Because no matter how badly your shoulder hurts now, most of your body's energy is going toward healing your wounds (they cut through your sternum when they do open heart surgery and wire it shut when they're done).

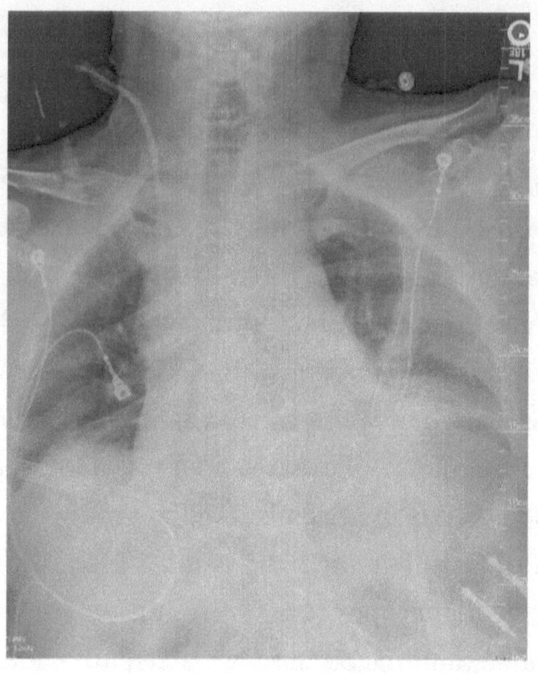

(See twist ties in X-Ray image and pacemaker wires
still intact.)

For almost the first three months after surgery,
my left shoulder hurt more than anything else.
Already having had a disabling bicycle accident in
1982, this was another disability to add to my poor
balance and poor bowel function and neurogenic
bladder.

Putting pants on. A belt. Washing my hair.
Reaching for the toothpaste. Brushing my teeth.

Moving around in bed. Using the ATM from the car. Three months after the surgery, all of these things were almost impossible and extremely painful. Then a CT Scan showed it wasn't a problem with the rotator cuff, which was when the orthopedist gave me a pain-relieving cortisone shot. I've since changed orthopedists and have learned I have "frozen shoulder," or "tight shoulder," or "shoulder impingement syndrome," which, now almost three years later, I'm apparently still recovering from.

Eventually, your energy will return to the extent that it can be directed toward other places on your body that need healing again. And there IS Hope! Now, nearly three years post-op, and I'm still working on my right shoulder.

LOVE

With Love From Rachel:

"My most memorable moment in the whole ordeal was when Chris was moved from the Cardiac Intensive Care floor to the Cardiac Step-down floor. That was when...

I Climbed Into Bed With Him.

At this point, he had a slim clear oxygen tube to his nostrils for breathing and an external pacemaker that looked like a throwback to the days of old transistor radios. It was the size of a Kleenex box, and it was connected to his heart by two slender wires. They went directly into his abdomen and were like delicate jumper cables.

Chris had these in him the whole time he was in the

hospital. It was a constant visual reminder to me that he could go at any minute.

After the trip to the cardiac step-down unit and meeting the nurses and doctors and aides. I. Shut. The. Door. (A delight.)

Chris moved to one side of the narrow hospital bed. He held out his arms to me. A wire with an oxygen monitor still hung from a finger.

I rejoiced as they disconnected each wire over the last several days in the hospital. Now, there were only the jumper cables and the finger monitor.

I took off my shoes and climbed ever so cautiously into bed with him. For me, this was coming home. More romantic than the Swiss Alps five months before. More romantic than his proposal with a horse-drawn carriage down to our neighborhood beach eight months before. I tried not to cry. Then, Chris started to cry. So, then, we both cried. And our bodies, with a rich history of casual daily intimacy, melted and relaxed into each other again like hands in gloves. Feet in socks. Heart to heart. I was back in my lover's arms and he was in mine. We shared loving comments that I don't recall. Soft laughter. Painful shifts of position. We curled around each other for several hours. Medical staff knocked and looked in, then smiled and left us alone to heal truly. The door was shut against the world."

We all need love, and when Rachel and I go to bed at night (once I could again make the climb up the stairs to the master bedroom), we go to bed with the one we love, and the one we love will take care of us as best they can no matter what.

"How much are you willing to do for each other?"

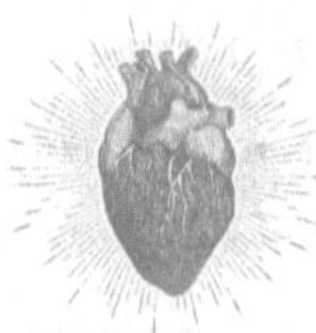

If you are married or with a significant other, and you're going through a critical medical emergency and recovery, then, with any hope, you are blessed to have your loved one or loved ones near.

If you are single, then hopefully you are blessed with friends and family and other loved ones.

If, for some reason, you do not have a lot of friends or family to visit and care for you and bring you things from their kitchen, then perhaps you are a member of a church or other organization that you can call on for help. Or talk to a social worker at the hospital or rehabilitation hospital.

If you're not a member of a church or organiza-tions, there are many churches that are willing to help hurting neighbors in times of need. But they require that you either reach out to them or that someone you know reach out to them so they know who you are, where you are, what you need when you need it and how they can get it to you.

These organizations are full of love. It is present and in abundance there, which I will discuss in the next chapter, and there is more of it than you can possibly know. People are, by and large, more than willing to help out someone who is in need.

Did I need to open my heart to let in more love?

I sometimes think I've had a lifetime of bullying. I was a tall, skinny kid whose "best friend" called me "bones" once from across a community pool area, leaving me mortified. But I continued across the pool area and told him what I thought. Other names that stick in my memory include bean pole, string bean, stilts, Lurch. (Some used the words in ways they thought were affectionate.)

Regardless, I carried on to high school where things were a bit easier. The hardest part was probably having to take showers at private high school in stalls that were not exactly private. I was so self-conscious as a kid; I can't begin to describe it.

So I was a bit low on confidence for most of my life. Various loving relationships helped me feel more confident, but self-consciousness has a way of getting between one's image of oneself and the good things other people say about you, no matter how good they feel.

Coming out of surgery and seeing my wife of three-and-a-half months there waiting for me to wake up, waiting for me to acknowledge her, waiting to exchange a glance, a touch, a wink, anything, I have to say, seemed amazing, terrifying, comforting, and relieving – all at the same time.

I was overtaken with 1.) A feeling that, Wow, she's here. This isn't too much for her. She has not given up. She is sticking with me. She cares! 2.) Oh, my God, how long is she going to be with me? How long is she going to put up with this? Even when I was home: Once I'm better, once I'm back on my feet, when will she realize, when will she tell me that she's had enough (yes, confidence, or lack thereof, is a powerful thing)? 3.) Whew, she's still here. She has even gathered members of my family and hers together, along with friends around her and around me to help.

Once I got back home, I saw the huge circle of love that included friends and family; people who brought things from our home to the hospital room; a friend who drove Rachel home in a snowstorm when she was so tired she was afraid to drive herself; family who brought us lasagna and stew they had made; my sister's Linzer torte; Pastor Shelley, who visited a couple of times and bringing a shawl that had been "packed with prayers" as it was knitted by members of the congregation at the church where she had married us three-and-a-half months earlier; offers of financial loans; and gifts. It was an outpouring that made me think that, if I had died, or if I do happen to die before Rachel does, she will have a large support group to hold her, comfort her, nurture her.

Not that this will make it easier … or will it?

I don't need to write something like Amy Krouse Rosenthal did in The New York Times article titled "You May Want to Marry My Husband" – a glowing review of her husband of 26 years, written days before she died after more than a year-long battle with ovarian cancer. (Google it.)

There are already plenty of people who know how wonderful Rachel is. I still can't believe that I am the luckiest man in the world because I get to have her as my wife. My life partner. Going to bed with her every night. Waking up with her every morning. Eating breakfast, lunch and dinner with her many days of the week. And everything else that goes with being married to the most beautiful woman in the world. I still can't believe it. I want to live a long time. And I want to love a long time.

When she reached the age of 40, Krouse Rosenthal asked how many more times she would get to look at a tree. Anything less than an infinite number of times more, she wrote, was too small and "not satisfactory." She said that she wanted to look at trees at least a million more times. And, no, that's not too much to ask. It might be too much to expect, but it's not too much to ask for. (https://www. nytimes.com/2017/03/13/style/amy-krouse-rosenthal-dies-modern-love.html) You just have to be prepared not to get that many. If it's even possible to be prepared.

One of the most amazing things that happened after the surgery was the number of voluntary offers for financial assistance we received. People offered us money, and others gave us money in get-well cards. "Just in case," one said. "Just to help." Other offers came in for loans. We didn't ask. They just came. Bottom line: We are blessed. And we know it. We know this does not happen to everyone, and we don't take that for granted. Not everyone is lucky enough to have such generous families or friends, or even to have families and friends able to be generous enough to offer such things. We have many friends, thanks to the beautiful community of which we are a part.

We have an abundance of friends and family,

love, generosity, thoughtfulness – all of which we see and for which we are grateful. Friends left quiche on our doorstep that sustained us when Rachel was driving back and forth to visit me in the hospital. Members of the church where we were married knitted the blanket "packed with prayers" that the minister delivered to my room. Family members stayed up all night praying. Others flew up from Florida and drove from New Jersey and New Hampshire just to be by my side and support Rachel with all she did.

No matter how you might feel three weeks after surgery – whether your back is starting to hurt again (it has since stopped), or your shoulder is starting to hurt again, or you feel tired all the time, and your bowels are not back to normal – no matter how you feel, if you think about it, chances are, if you live in the United States, you're probably living a life of abundance and have more to be grateful for than most people who consider themselves "healthy," and who haven't just come out of open-heart surgery or whatever other major procedure you might be recovering from.

Just some back story: My shoulder hurt before the surgery. I haven't been able to play golf for a couple of years. It's a game I can't even say I'm mediocre at, though I still enjoy the occasional good shot that I make. A good tee shot. A good fairway shot to the green close to the cup. A good putt up and down undulations of the green close to or into the cup. These are the things that used to keep me coming back to the course to spend $20-$30 for a few hours of, well, golf.

After the surgery, my shoulder hurt worse than it ever had. It was like having another disability. It was hard to imagine having limited use of both arms. I use my hands and arms a lot to balance, to pull up my pants, put on a belt, put on a shirt, dry myself after a shower, wash my hair, brush my teeth. These are things most people use their arms for. I also use them to balance going up and down the stairs and for balance while taking a shower.

My left shoulder hurt so much in the weeks and months after my surgery that I couldn't lean against that one when I was taking a shower. And I need to be able to lean against it because 1) I'm right-handed and 2) Because I lost a good deal of my balance when I became disabled in 1982. So it helps to lean on things to keep me steady.

I spent the first month or so downstairs sleeping (on my back) and resting in our guest bedroom. I would, of course, get up and walk around as much as

I could. It was nearly impossible to put on a belt, pull up my pants, brush my teeth, wash my hair, turn over in bed, sleep on my side, open jars, really almost anything that involved putting pressure on my left arm in any way. It wasn't even because they had sawed through my sternum, and that was still healing.

I went to see an orthopedist about it less than three months after surgery. He asked me how long it had been since my surgery. When I said three months, his facial expression seemed to express that it had been too soon to be able to tell whether it was just the shoulder giving me problems or if it was too soon since the surgery to say. So I gave it another month before getting a cortisone shot, which has given me almost complete relief. It was about three months after the heart surgery that I opted for the cortisone. Six months later, I could once again turn over in bed, climb on the bed to kiss my wife, pull up my pants, reach for the toothpaste with my left arm. I could even swing a golf club halfway decently, although I have yet to test that theory at the driving range or on a golf course.

I've known somewhat intuitively, somewhat by way of being in a loving relationship with Rachel, that there is such a thing as an abundance mentality.

Confession: I don't have it. At least I didn't have it. Although I think I have it more now. Much more. Even though Rachel might attest to me still being a negative Nelly, or an Eeyore. Though I'm not that pessimistic, gloomy or depressed, nor do I have a detachable tail with a pink bow on the end of it, I am sometimes not confident of my literacy and have tried to write poems (Eeyore is the only Pooh character who has ventured into the literary writing, citing not biting while fighting how exciting).

Now I am alive. I am not dead. I am glad to be alive. It's good to be alive, and we're glad I didn't die. These are truths we actually tell each other fairly often. Rachel is glad I am alive. I have a repaired aorta. I have a repaired valve. The surgeon said he expects a full recovery. I know I'll probably need a replacement in 8-12 years that will probably be done by way of a minimally invasive procedure of some sort, perhaps through trans-arterial valve replacement (TAVR), or hologram, who knows?

To continue. I have accomplished a lot. I have received trophies and awards as a child and as an adult. I have been recognized by my peers for the work that I have done. One person said I saved their life. That's pretty good. Anyone should feel complete knowing they saved someone's life, shouldn't they? I have changed people's lives. I have affected people's lives. I made the woman at the drugstore laugh a real laugh tonight. I have laughed more with Rachel than I think I have in my whole life. These are signs of abundance. Abundance of love, of laughter, of family, of friends, of wealth (material and, more importantly, spiritual), of attitude and gratitude.

I think Jimmy Buffet should consider recasting his lyrics to say: "Changes in attitude, changes in gratitude. If we couldn't laugh, we would all go insane." That would certainly be fitting for me – more on that in the "G" chapter.

REMEMBER:

Hospitals have patient advocates who can refer patients to social services in their area. Check on this, if you can, before going into the hospital. In emergencies, it won't be possible to do this in advance, but then your doctors and nurses should be able to help you find organizations that can be of assistance after your discharge from the hospital.

Nursing homes are convalescent centers where people go to recover from surgery for as long as needed. If you have insurance, this could be a cheaper option if you don't have any other place to go than a hotel or motel. If you don't have a home to go back to (some people have to stop work, lose their income, can't pay their rent, etc.), then call your Center for Independent Living (CIL). Have your social worker at the hospital look them up and put you in contact with them. They can be an invaluable resource!

If you know you can go home after your surgery, try to make some preparations at home before you go, if possible.

Telephone charging cables. Make sure you have them where you will need them. This can save a lot of trouble when you're back home. Other things that you have in your bedroom that give you comfort. For me, it's earplugs, headphones, pillows, books and my Kindle (http://kindle.com).

Get extra pillows ready. Get clothes ready and laid out. Get your pajamas out. Put some bottled water and snacks close to the bed or where someone can find them to bring them to you. I like bags of trail mix and crackers. These may not be the healthiest of snacks, but we all have our guilty pleasures, don't we?

If you can, and if you will need one, get a shower bench and set it up before you're discharged. Have a walker ready if you're going to need one or even if it might come in handy.

Program your emergency numbers and contacts on your phone. Give someone you know well an extra key to your house in case you need to call on them. See if you can find someone who will call you or come in to check on you at regular times during the week.

You might be eligible for visits from the Visiting Nurse Association, or VNA. Check with them before going into the hospital or before being discharged.

UNDERSTANDING

I said several times, "I'm sorry." I felt sorry for having put Rachel through so much turmoil and trouble and difficulty and worry. I was sorry I had put everyone through so much. I was grateful my parents made the trip from Florida to see me, but I felt bad that they felt they had to come up to see me one more time before I either died (or lived). When I said, "Sorry," Rachel would say, "Don't apologize. And thanks for staying with me."

The human mind can understand that which it can grasp for if it cannot grasp something in order to understand, then understanding is out of reach. To grasp something one must first be able to reach it, either with their hands or perhaps only with their eyes – to grasp it with their eyes, to hold it in their sight or view, might be to hold it within their sight as an apparition, but not a phantom for phantoms are not made to be understood.

Phantoms are made NOT to be understood, or else they would not be called phantoms, or ghosts, or spirits, or wraiths, unless they be in the shape of a sponge or an empty container that can hold something, lest it not be a container to contain including a thought molecule or however many molecules it takes to contain a thought to constitute a memory or something learned, but for now the human mind seeks understanding until we arrive at a oneness of mind in the universe, a noosphere. Then perhaps we will know inherently, instinctively, but, until then, we must be satisfied with knowing only that which we can grasp, that which we can hold in our hands, or in our sight, including in our hearts and minds.

The room was dark many a night while I thought about what was in my chest – my heart, newly repaired, surgically, awakening to a deeper love than I had ever known from anyone other than perhaps my mother. But it was a spousal, not filial love.

I came to feel that I understood what Rachel was saying on an intellectual level, but only later would I come around to understanding it fully with my heart and soul and my mind.

Post-surgery depression brought on by the facing of one's mortality is something doctors generally do not warn their patients about. Chronic pain, reactions to pain killers, anesthesia. These are all factors, or can be, in post-surgery depression. Symptoms can include excessive sleeping, irritability and moodiness, general fatigue, anxiety, stress, or hopelessness, and loss of appetite.

Depression after heart surgery is so common it has its own name – "cardiac depression" – and according to the American Heart Association, and others, up to 33% of those who undergo cardiac surgery will experience some degree of cardiac depression.

https://www.heart.org/HEARTORG/
HealthyLiving/StressManagement/
HowDoesStressAffectYou/Depression-After-A-
Cardiac-Event-or-
Diagnosis_UCM_440444_Article.jsp

The understanding that I write about here isn't the kind that you would expect to find in most books. I don't want to understand you, the reader. At least not in this book at this time. What I am hoping for is for each of us who have been through a crisis or crises, or who may at some point go through a crisis (don't we all at some point or another deal with a crisis? – a death in the family, or of a friend, or simply being alone can be considered a crisis) – I hope for each of us to have a better understanding of where we are, where we have come from and where we are going. I wish for these crisis-experiencers to know what to do when they find themselves thrust into a crisis for which they were unprepared. I want them to know who they can turn to and what to ask for. I want their understanding to be as complete as possible.

"The only moment we have is now."

It might sound I because the mind struggles to grasp it. Most do, anyway. The Now. We read about it when others write about it. We hear about it when others discuss it. But when we say it, do we understand it? The Now?

Let me tell you, and I may be repeating myself here, when you're being wheeled into the operating room, waving goodbye to your loved one(s), or even just thinking that this may be it, that this may be the last time you see the lights of a hospital, feel the warmth of a heated blanket against your skin, the soft kiss of your wife's lips and warm touch of her hand on yours and the way her amazing eyes look when they gaze into yours, even if they are welling up with tears, that's when it's too late to learn what "now" means.

When your life flashes before your eyes, that's when it's too late.

The answer to the questions: What am I grateful for? And When am I grateful? Is the same – Now.

When a crisis comes, then it's too late. For me, January of 2017 almost was too late. I was afraid that the future I had imagined for myself would evaporate if I didn't get to work on it soon. The life I had now, the repaired aorta, the replaced valve, could be gone tomorrow, or in an instant.

But, now, this time, I knew I had survived, but ... and when I think of some way to vocalize what I'm feeling existentially, all I can come up with is: "What if?"

What if I hadn't come out on this side but on the other side?

What if that had been the last time?

What if the sight of my last smile as I was being wheeled into surgery was the last smile my wife had seen?

What if she had been left with all my papers?

All my computer files?

All the books I'd read and had planned to read?

All my email contacts to let know I was passed on to a less painful, more peaceful place?

What if?

What if I hadn't gotten to see my parents again?

What if ... my brother and sisters?

My best friends?

My circle of friends.

"All of a sudden." "We didn't know he was sick." "We didn't know he had heart problems." "We didn't expect any of this would ever happen to him." "He was such a great guy." "Blah blah blah." It's all words at that point. It's all just words. What can be said, really? What can be said, other than I love you, or goodbye?

So, I say, if you're waiting for life to peak... like, as an example, "getting my book published will be great." Getting that manager position. Getting that next raise. Getting that next job.

These are, or can be, highlights. But, please, remember, the greatest moment is Now. No matter what else is happening. Now is all there is.

There's no other way to look at it, and there's no other way to say it, and it just doesn't get any more simple or complicated than that.

It just is, and we have to learn it and accept it and live with it and maybe, even, die with it.

Since we have to be ready to die at any moment, every moment has to be our best. And each moment can be full of intense gratitude.

There's no other better way that I know of to say it, and there's no more important thing that I can think of to try to communicate in these pages. To understand the NOW better than before is one reward for all that flirtation with eternity that I got and for which I'm eternally grateful. Now to hold on to that and practice it!

Gratitude is the choice to see and attend to what is good in the midst of the chaos. It is also a sense of enduring thankfulness.

Of course, I'm glad to be alive. I'm grateful. One of my favorite bands is the Grateful Dead. Well, you could say I'm among the grateful living. As I wrote to a friend of mine about five weeks after the surgery:

"That's a beautiful remembrance (http://peacenews.org/2017/02/09/joyce-rawitscher-words-remembrance). Glad no one has had to do that for me yet!"

I'm still a tad "discontent" when I think about it. Thinking about it is what I've done a little of the first few weeks and months after surgery because I have a few unfulfilled dreams (not an unfulfilled life mind you).

"Probably every generation sees itself as charged with remaking the world. Mine, however, knows it will not remake the world. Its task is even greater: to keep the world from destroying itself." ~ Albert Camus

I still feel I'm trying to sort it all out. Intellectually and emotionally.

My bike accident in 1982 seems like a long time ago. That almost killed me, and my life was altered in many ways forever. I think my energies at that time went, over the next five-to-ten years, toward recovery and college and getting into the workforce.

I lost a month or two back then when I was 18 years old. I don't remember them. I was hit on July 2. I woke up, sort of, around August four weeks after being hit by a car. I had been in intensive care in Omaha for four weeks and remember bits and pieces of that. I was 18 going on 19. I really only remember a few days of ICU. I remember convincing the doctor not to tie me to the bed while I was on dialysis after my kidneys failed. I remember pulling the shunt out of my arm when he left the room. I remember a nurse working to replace the shunt and keep me from bleeding to death. I remember telling my cycling coach during a visit he made to the ICU during his honeymoon that I wanted still to ride my bike cross-country. That, he said, "might be tempting the gods."

Once I was out of ICU and at Hartford Hospital, back in my home state of Connecticut, I remember constantly complaining that it felt like my feet were on fire. The hospital staff tried in vain to comfort me. Nothing worked.

I remember asking the doctor when the pain in my backside – where I had been hit by the Chevy Blazer driven by a 19-year-old Nebraskan – would go away. "It will never go away," he said, "you're just going to get used to it." My sister, an artist, made me a birthday card. The card was on a piece of paper that must have been 6-feet wide. I squinted and tried as hard as I could to read it. While I couldn't read it, I knew what it was, and I said: "Thank You."

Come September of that year, I was at a rehabilitation hospital. Then I think the point of daily life was survival and getting myself to the point where I could move out of the house again and live independently.

My parents told me that social workers explained to them how events like this often destroy marriages.

"It almost did," my father recounts. "At the time we thought it might. But it didn't. Everything worked out. You got better, and that's what's important."

But remembering being rolled away on a stretcher into the operating room in January of 2017, kissing my wife of three-and-a-half months, possibly for the last time, and deciding to smile to her, or for her, albeit through the tears, while waving, yes, waving goodbye, gives me a sense of urgency to the goal of living a meaningful, fulfilling, accomplished life, or at least, to begin with, to identifying exactly what that means. Now.

What makes a meaningful, fulfilling, accomplished life?

One of the most difficult parts of this entire ordeal, in fact, was waving goodbye to my wife not knowing if I would come back out on this side of life, and see her again or whether I'd have to wait for her in the afterlife or watch her from heaven crying and grieving and help her along in life without me. It was a moment I hadn't expected. So it is even more surprising when that moment stirs more emotion than any surrounding this "event."

All we knew when they wheeled me away was that they were going to look at my aorta from inside my throat. If there was going to be surgery, and they were pretty sure there would be, it would either be four or six hours.

I remember waking up in a room with people in the blue-green hospital scrubs wearing surgical masks and (I could not speak with the breathing tube in at this point) thinking "If this is heaven, it looks an awful lot like the inside of a hospital."

I still wasn't sure, though. Even though I was waking up in a place that looked like a hospital or operating room or ICU, I wasn't convinced that I had come through without dying. I was simply aware that wherever I was looked like a hospital.

Even when I saw my wife, my thoughts were similar.

"Does this mean I made it?"

But the possibility that I had indeed made it made tears well up in my eyes. Perhaps my belief that we just continue, or seem to continue once we've died, was true, and I was in heaven. Perhaps I am now, although it has become quite clear that I have settled back into my old life. But who's to say what death is like, or the afterlife, if there is one? Who's to say that it's not exactly like the life we're living now, just sort of continued like a dream?

I walk out of a dentist's appointment, before which I'm supposed to pre-medicate now to prevent any germs from entering my bloodstream through my gums. There are an ambulance and a police car with their lights rolling and flashing. "Are these for me?" I wonder surrealistically, as I walk by gingerly. Grateful that they seem not to be.

So, what does it mean? When I was 18, I set out as a recent high school graduate, to take a year off and ride my bicycle cross country. I went, in part, to educate citizens who were willing to listen – mostly members of schools and church groups – about the dangers of nuclear war and nuclear fall-out. I encouraged them to make their towns designated "green zones." Back then, it was to save the world – to help rid the world of nuclear weapons that would destroy the atmosphere and make it impossible for anyone to live on this planet for any length of time. Towns are still signing resolutions to avoid the prospect in their locales. (http://masspeaceaction. org/somerville-passes-resolution-a-call-to-prevent- nuclear-war).

Back then, that was the most important thing,

especially for this 18-year-old. Plus, riding my bike across the country wasn't so bad either! I still think that to reduce the number of nuclear weapons, and weapons, in general, is a very important step we can take, and perhaps one of the most urgent and important ones everyone can make, in the world today. We've known for generations that the military-industrial complex is the richest sector of the economy and that more than half our tax dollars fund it every year. We know that most of the rulers of the countries in the world profit from the military and oil industries. We've known and have so far failed to do anything about it.

There's not much news or information about STOP Nuclear War on the Internet, though some of the letters published in "Reagan: A Life in Letters" do mention the organization. Students wrote in asking the president for Reagan's response to claims that were made by STOP and other international peace and disarmament organizations. He, of course, belittled the "fact sheets" that quoted numbers of weapons, numbers of those who would die, etc., and said it saddened him that teachers were spreading misinformation.

There is also an article in Education Week in

which my old cycling coach is quoted. In another, his wife is attributed as being the program director of STOP Nuclear War.

I'm glad to see STOP Nuclear War listed among a slew of other national and international organizations still working to prevent nuclear war, and working to educate the public and politicians about the dangers of nuclear war – especially since most politicians who support the modernization of current nuclear stockpiles probably don't understand how many times over the population of the planet could be eliminated with the size and numbers of weapons that our global neighbors and we currently have around the world). But I digress…

Gratitude is the opposite of guilt, and it is received by others better than guilt is. "Thank you for being there for me. Thank you for sticking with me. Thank you for all you've done." Any of these are received better than "I'm sorry for what I've put you through." Maybe one "I'm sorry" is alright. But stop after one.

One thing I learned through the healing process, at least as an adult, is that your sorrow and your grief are your own creations. They can turn into gratitude. Thank someone for doing something for you, taking care of you, checking on you, sending you a card, thinking of you. Once I realized that Rachel and I were both going through something that I had no, or little control over, it was easier to make that transition in thought. It was easier to see that I hadn't done anything and that it wasn't my fault. What had happened to me and what I was going through and what Rachel was now having to go through and deal with: They were not my fault. (And neither was the bicycle accident, but that is for another book.)

After my cycling accident, my parents were angry and said things to me about what I put them through. Granted, it's sometimes tough to be a parent, and we do the best we can do with what we're given. Sometimes our kids get hurt, fall out of trees, break a leg. Sometimes, God forbid, they die before we do. I've almost died a couple of times, and I'm grateful I've lived to tell the tales; to see another Christmas, wedding anniversary; Easter; birthday; autumn. Everything. I'm glad I've survived to see everything again. The ocean. The birds. The trees. Even when I think about it, to feel the pain. I have to be grateful because it's a sign I'm alive.

"They told us on several occasions to not expect anything, that you might not make it through the night," my parents told me about my ICU stay in 1982. Doctors attributed my survival largely to my having been in such good shape after having been a varsity cyclist for three years and to having pedaled a thousand miles or so, 65-110 miles a day for the previous 2-3 weeks. I had made decisions that put me in that place where that happened, but I was not to blame. My parents eventually learned this, as did I.

Where I'm going with this is that we all, or at least most of us, have some sense of guilt put upon us by those who raise us. They invest a lot of time and love in our safety, well being, education, and other things, and we should be grateful (not do things that might screw that up). We don't do any of those things that might screw that up on purpose, of course. We might say we do things out of anger. Run away from home. Attempt suicide even. But that's not really because of our parents. There are things that happen within us that control our decisions to do things, good or bad.

Even if it seems like someone we know – a child or a friend – is doing something to harm themselves intentionally, there is probably something more behind it. Drugs and mental illness have been shown to be the cause of more suicides than pure anger or spite. Even if victims have depression or are being treated with medication, they often are not able to know or see what the consequences of their actions will be before they act.

I was a teenager on a mission in 1982. I was a cyclist who was free to see the country and meet its people, all while riding my bike as part of the Pilgrimage for Peace. I was living the life!

But I did not do any of those things knowing that I was going to make anyone's lives any more difficult than I already had since having been born. Nonetheless, they were hurt, probably fearful, and angry, and that came out at times directed toward me. Just as I understand my own human failings, I try to understand those of others, especially the ones I love.

Once, much later in life, when I was well on in my journalism career, I met a psychologist as part of a story I was working on about Greater Hartford's Volunteers In Psychotherapy program (http://www. ctvip.org). I naturally began to talk about my life and that I had never seen a psychologist about dealing with issues of loss and anger related to that bicycling accident. Well, little did I know that I would learn something from that meeting. Why are you angry? Why are your parents angry? Whose fault was all this that happened? It wasn't your fault, was it? These are questions I recall being asked to address in myself. I didn't realize I was going to get my own session.

It wasn't my fault. After all these years, it wasn't my fault! On occasion, I still told them I was sorry it happened. I actually think they either matured faster than I did, or they got more psychological counseling than I did. They didn't always spew angry comments to me about the accident. Over time they seemed to come to terms with the fact that it wasn't my fault faster than I did.

Know that it's not your fault

Following my emergency heart surgery, I cried myself to sleep many nights in our guest bedroom downstairs, repeating over and over, "It's not my fault. It wasn't my fault. It's not my fault. It wasn't my fault." And on and on and on. My broken aorta and weak valve and the emergency were not my fault. I knew this, but I was still riddled with guilt that I had messed up the launching of Rachel's studies that year. That I had used up so much of so many people's time.

Some of those nights, I would have nightmares or

"stress dreams." They would either be about someone breaking into the house or someone doing something to piss me off. I would wake both of us up. In my dream, I'd be saying things like, "Go away!" or "Fuck off." But in real life, I'd just be moaning or yelling, "Aaaargh." I think it took about six months, but I'm grateful now that these seem to have lessened, and my dreams are interesting once again.

I felt so guilty and so sorry for the pain and suffering and doubt and worry and grief and fear that my wife took on. Mind you; I didn't say "what I put her through," though that is how I felt at the time.

I felt that I was putting her through something that she would have never in a million years chosen to deal with. But we had married three-and-a-half months prior. We had spoken to the minister about things that might happen and what we would be willing to do. It was made quite clear that we would probably, at some point – albeit we never imagined it would be this soon – at some point that we would be responsible for caring for the other.

I was sorry. I was so sorry. I felt I had not taken care of myself. I had somehow not read an echo-cardiogram report closely enough. I had gone to the wrong doctor or something. I had done *something* wrong that caused this stress on my heart to damage the aorta and create the need for emergency open-heart surgery.

With tears dripping into my ears on one side and down my face on the other side, while lying on my back in bed, I muttered myself to sleep with the words: "It wasn't my fault. It wasn't my fault. It wasn't my fault. It wasn't my fault." Eventually, I felt a cloud of gratitude surrounding me, enveloping me, swallowing me, comforting me.

That cloud would come around again one night while remembering, thinking, contemplating, measuring what I had been through. What we had been through. How far we had come. All that we had dealt with. With ourselves and with each other.

Even though she didn't hear the muttering, she heard the guilt. Eventually, Rachel said, "Shut up with that guilt shit. It wasn't your fault. I know you wouldn't have chosen this." And I wouldn't have. Obviously. No one would.

Rachel, of course, was right. It wasn't my fault. I knew it wasn't my fault. Something in the way I had been programmed, something in my past, made me feel bad about what had happened. I'm over it. For the most part, at least. I'm not sure I'll ever be completely over it. But I can accept the fact that it wasn't my fault and that I would have done the same thing, devoted the same amount of time and energy and resources to helping Rachel improve had something happened to her that landed her in the ICU.

HOPE

As Brené Brown is often quoted as saying, "Hope is not an emotion, but a thought process made up of goals, pathways and agency." Hope happens, she says, when we can set goals and can pursue them and believe in ourselves. C. R. Snyder, Brown notes, also found that hope is learned. (https://onbeing.org/programs/1-courage-born-struggle-brene-brown)

"When boundaries, consistency, and support are in place, children learn hope from their parents. But even if we didn't get it as kids, we can still learn hope as adults. It's just tougher because we have to resist and unlearn old habits, like the tendency to give up when things get tough.

"Hope is a function of struggle," she says. "If we're never allowed to fall or face adversity as children, we are denied the opportunity to develop the tenacity and sense of agency we need to be hopeful."

Hope and optimism teach us that things will get better. They will improve.

There are those who are forever discontent, dissatisfied for there is always so much more that needs to be done. With the election of a reality television host and bankruptcy expert and one-time porn film extra as president of the United States of America, there is a sense of hopelessness that leads some of us to strive to do bigger and better things to end the injustices that we feel we can see. Personally, I like to deconstruct these distressing events, whether that be through poetry, song, protest, meditation, or prayer.

I found out shortly after leaving the hospital that my client, Herb, never did move out of the nursing home. On the day he was to move out, the day the scheduled transportation showed up at his nursing home to take him to his new apartment, Herb decided to stay in the nursing home.

Living independently, which is what my colleagues and I try very hard to help our consumers do, wasn't for him. Looking back, thinking of all that had happened while working with him, it didn't surprise me or anyone who knew him, really. We had moved in his furniture. The lease was ready to be signed. The ride showed up. But Herb decided to stay in bed that day and not move to the brand new apartment with ADA features and affordable rent we had lined up for him.

But there is always hope. Hope for me was a soup in which I was bathing from the moment I called my wife from the car in the pouring rain. Before I spotted the gleaming lights of the Mobil gas station, Subway sandwich shop, and Dunkin' Donuts. It kicked in.

I hope this is going to be alright. I hope the ambulance gets here on time. I hope I know what they're doing. I hope we get to the hospital on time. I hope I don't need anything serious. I hope ... Et cetera. It went on and on to the point where the anesthesiologist was placing the mask on my face. Hope is a prayer. Hope, at least, accompanies a prayer.

I hope this isn't my last memory, however brief this memory is, I hope it is not my last and that I can come back and create more, many more even more beautiful memories with my wife, my family, and my friends and everyone else who might want to be, or who I might want to be part of my memories.

For me, thinking about the what-ifs was, and

sometimes still is, the hardest part of the post-operative cycle.

For Rachel, "Hope is a white kitten, padding through the snow." She explains how it has to do with the ephemeral nature we hope we see.

"When things are really bad, and you think you see a white kitten in the snow, it gives you a sense of hope that there really is a kitten, warm and snuggly. Like an oasis in the desert," she says.

There was a good deal of hopefulness for Rachel in the possibility of my getting the breathing tube removed, getting the drainage tubes removed, being able to go downstairs and do a load of laundry myself, go upstairs and sleep in the master bedroom, starting cardio-rehab, driving, and other things that would improve my daily life while recovering from this surgery.

For Rachel, they were handholds and footholds on her way up the wall that she imagined climbing while sitting by my side as I got well enough to go home from the hospital, and, then, sitting by my side, or nearby at home while I got well enough to fend for myself.

Rachel says she experienced the whole thing almost like a rock climber, striving to reach for the next firm rock to tap in each small shiny piton. ("In climbing, a piton is a metal spike (usually steel) that is driven into a crack or seam in the climbing surface with a climbing hammer." They act as anchors to protect the climber from falling or to assist the climbing process. https://en.wikipedia. org/wiki/Piton.)

Because of the work I've done, I'm very familiar with shower chairs and walkers. But when they brought a walker into my room that was for me to take home, I thought, "What? When am I ever going to use that?" I actually didn't use the walker. Over the years, I've become pretty good at using walls and trim in the house to help keep my balance.

And then there was the shower chair. I did use the shower chair for a few weeks until I started going upstairs to the master bedroom to sleep and use the master bath to take showers. Perhaps I should have continued to use it, but I was determined to do a few things – get away from sitting in the shower, get back to a normal diet that produced normal bowel movements, get back to taking a shower every day (and not just to warm my feet up at night or in the morning), and, really, just get back to my normal lifestyle that I was used to before all this happened.

I was determined to get to the point where I

wasn't afraid of busting loose the Dacron used to patch up my aorta while straining too much, whether that was lifting something or straining too much doing something else. And I was determined to get back to bouncing down the stairs without feeling my heart bouncing around in my chest. Two years later, my abdominal CT scan showed things are stable. I was still having thoughts of busting what was fixed. Or flossing my teeth too much and infecting the valve. But two years after the surgery the surgeon said things are stable and the cardiologist says not to worry.

While I was in surgery other pitons for Rachel included: not breaking down until the surgery was over and before calling family members.

It was after midnight. Chris had been wheeled into the emergency operating room about 90 minutes prior. The nurse came out and handed me his wedding ring (Don't break down. Don't break down.) The surgeon came out later and said, "it's what we thought – an aortic dissection," and he discussed with me calmly the medical pros and cons of a metal valve (longer-lasting) vs. a biological valve (no coumadin). The discussion was totally surreal. We had only been married for about three months. So, to have this choice to make on his behalf, which would affect the rest of his life – or not, if he didn't make it through this emergency surgery – was baffling and grave. Plus, what did I know of the pros and cons of various valves? Still, I made my choice.

A while after that, my sister Julia arrived. (Another piton.) I had called her, not being able to speak much, mostly crying. She said, "I'll come." And she brought all the cell phone chargers she could find in the house. Amazing Sisterhood.

I was curled up under my coat on a hard hospital couch in a very large room when she arrived. Of course, we hugged. Of course, I sobbed.

"When did you last eat?" she asked. I couldn't remember. (The next day, I got home to see that I had been midway through making some pasta and sauce for our dinner when Chris had called in a panic the night before.)

Julia and I took the elevator from the cardiac surgical waiting room to the hospital atrium. We had my purse, my coat, all of Chris' clothes, his backpack, his coat, all of Julia's belongings as well. We piled them by a table in the atrium next to the all-night hospital cafeteria. It was bleaker than Hopper's "Nighthawks at the Diner."(https://en.wikipedia.org/wiki/Nighthawks_(painting)*)*

I got up first and got a tuna sandwich and some kind of herbal tea. (Another piton. Eating.) I sat back down next to the large pitiful pile of belongings. Julia got up, rubbed my back for a moment, and went to get some food for herself.

That's when Chris appeared to me. He was standing about 12 feet up in the air, looking down at me. He was naked, perfect and radiant. He was smiling. I knew I was in the hospital atrium, with a sandwich in front of me. I also knew this was really Chris before me. It was the same level of knowing as the hours in the emergency room, the conversations with the surgeons, the calls to his family and mine, the glossy green plants of the atrium. We emanated love for each other.

I asked him, "Will you stay?"

He asked me, "Do you want me to stay?"

I replied, "Yes, I want you to stay!"

Then, I was up in the air with him. Both of us naked and beautiful. We held hands with our arms outstretched creating a circle between us and surrounding us. It was a perfect loving moment. I seemed to break the enchantment by asking him "Why is this happening?" Chris seemed to shrug or have difficulty answering and he faded away. My certainty that he would make it through surgery and beyond was sustained because of this vision.

Later, I pieced together that this was probably the moment when they found Chris' ruptured aorta. The brilliant work of the surgeon saved him from bleeding to death on the operating table. And Chris decided to stay, because I asked him to.

"We had some difficult moments," *the surgeon told me. (This discussion was another piton. Chris made it through the surgery, fully alive.)*

A rupture is "rare" and "extremely dangerous." An aortic rupture that close to the heart can empty the blood from a body in seconds.

But because of the atrium visitation, at some level, I knew all would be well. Later events, like seeing him with all the tubes and wires, gave me momentary doubts. But at the soul level, I had a sustained knowing that all would be well.

When I told our friend Pat, a shaman who co-offici-ated our wedding ceremony, she said the visitation was our "spiritual wedding." And so it is. I don't need any more ceremony though!

Other post-surgery pitons included: getting the morphine level high enough to relieve his pain. (I remem-bered that scene in the movie "Terms of Endearment," when Shirley MacLaine's character pounds on the nurse's desk saying "It's time for the pain meds!!!"

We got a daily treatment plan. I continued to main-tain my calm and not freak out. I kept from screaming and not assuming a fetal position on the sofa. We were winning.

They told me getting through the surgery was the first important survival step.

The second survival step was making it past the first four hours post-op.

Then, the first 24 hours.

Getting the breathing tubes removed.

Chris coming out of sedation.

My goals were to 1. Be strong, 2. Show the hospital staff that Chris has an advocate. 3. Be appreciative. 4. Ask questions. 5. Get Chris to shift positions regularly, drink lots of water, eat lots of good food. Comfort and support him.

Other pitons: phone calls to family and friends, trying to act reassuring. Trying to be gracious and informative to family members arriving from as far away as Florida, New Jersey, New Hampshire. Not yelling at the nurses when I saw the pain Chris was in when they took him from the bed and put him in a chair.

Daily schedule pitons:

- *Get out of bed.*
- *Call the intensive care nurses station without screaming: "IS HE STILL ALIVE?!?"*
- *Cry in the shower.*
- *Eat something. (Who gave us that quiche?*

Daily slice of quiche was a godsend.) Stay with Chris (for about 12 hours every day).

- *Drink some herbal tea that will support me (thanks Nina! I told her name and brand and aisle at the supermarket. A great friend in need.)*
- *Get the car. (Hospital valet, also a godsend.)*
- *Drive home.*
- *Eat something.*
- *Get into bed.*
- *Cry.*
- *Sleep.*
- *Get up.*
- *Call the intensive care nurse's station, again without screaming.*
- *Be strong for Chris.*

Rachel writes more:

Every day in the hospital was both tedious and stress-ful. I strove to be available to Chris, knowing the high level of pain and disorientation he was experiencing. However, I also knew that I needed to run this marathon and not focus on the sprint of the day.

Waking up at home alone and realizing the house is cold. Why turn on the heat when I'm just leaving as soon as I can? Wow, I just had a thought that wasn't about Chris. I call the ICU. He's okay. I eat two slices of quiche. My appetite is returning. I see a connection between my own energy levels and Chris' healing. A heartfelt connection. I'm hungry, which must mean I'm less worried, right?

What day is it?

How long have we been here?

It's like reporting to work. With no pay. Back to the salt mines. I really couldn't be anywhere else but right by Chris' bedside.

The surgeon comes in again, "you're a lucky man, Mr. Zurcher!" I rustle through some things, so I don't weep openly. The surgeon is such a good man.

"Do you want more water? Do you want more to eat? Do you want to try the chair for a while? I can help you stand and shift. I've got you," the surgeon says to Chris. And that's beautiful. (But who's got me? I wonder. Waking to my own needs at last.)

What do I need? What do I need? I learn a little bit about how to ask for help. Friends bring me green *drinks, teas, quiche, snow boots, and sandwiches. When people show up to visit Chris, I go down to the atrium and walked laps like a crazy person. I decide that I don't need to watch the removals of the various tubes or various procedures. I leave and walk more laps in the atrium.*

My friend JoAnne told me about "circles of care" when describing her child's medical crisis. The person experiencing the crisis is in the center of the circle. One or two intimates offer care to Chris (that's me).

So, I give care to Chris and myself. The next circle around us is immediate family and close friends. Their role is to give care to Chris and me. Perhaps one of them offers to be a communication conduit for the rest of them. (Chris' brother Tom did this for us!) Then, there is the broader circle of friends. They need to get their emotional comfort from each other, not Chris or me. I can't be the one to give them directions on how to get to the hospital. If they wish to give us food, they need to drop it off – not ask me to pick it up.

My boundaries are clearer, and I ask friends and family to get their answers elsewhere.

This "circle of care" image was so helpful to me. It gave me permission to take care of Chris and myself. It was helpful to ignore texts or emails from people who wanted daily updates, but couldn't offer support. I got to decide how much energy I had for visits, for communications, for phone calls.

I asked for people to take walks with me in the atrium. I told people that Chris was not up for a visit. I asked people to shorten their visit. I made sure I ate breakfast calmly in the mornings. I used the hospital valet parking service, so I wouldn't have to remember where I parked. I decided that I would not be a good social person. I would be there for Chris and for myself.

The one time that I did not follow this rule was early on, when Chris' brother and sister-in-law and my sister and her family, and my parents were all at the hospital in the waiting room together. It was very early on, and I stayed with everyone socializing.

I found out later that Chris was in pain and needed help changing the position of the hospital bed. He couldn't get a nurse fast enough, and when I came back into the room, he asked that I not leave him alone for more than 10 minutes at a time. That made it clear to me that I sometimes needed to be "not nice" so that I could support Chris in his recovery.

Two days after open-heart surgery, they wanted him to walk. Are they nuts?

But, he walks. He's using a walker and wearing the johnny coat to the nurse's station (10 feet away) and back. On the way there, I check out his ass. On the walk back, I *see the exhaustion in his eyes. But, yes, he's walking. Another level climbed.*

Pastor Shelly called and visited, bringing a shawl packed with prayers from all who helped knit it. Thank you, Church of the Redeemer friends! I wore the shawl and I put it on Chris' legs.

I called Chris' family every morning and night. Although I remember that Chris doesn't want me to leave him for more than 10 minutes, I decide that I need to walk and shut down his needs for a little bit. Coming back to the room, he's okay.

At times, I push the hospital staff for more meds. To change sheets. To look at an IV site. Instead of just being nice, I become a strong (respectful) advocate. As a result, the great doctors and nurses consult me, and they offer blankets, ice, kind words, updates, and plans. I could call the ICU desk after I drove home, and first thing when I woke up for status reports. These actions were so helpful to me as I managed my own worries and rest schedule.

More pitons included a little less crying in the morning. A little less crying in the evening. The morning I came into the hospital room and Chris was up sitting in the chair eating fruit. He smiled at me.

What a wonderful, beautiful gorgeous moment! This is good. We can do this.

Kathy H. delivers my winter boots following a snow-

storm. Jack P. offers a ride home in the snow – do I go home? Do I stay overnight?

"Well, if you were my wife, I'd tell you to shut up and get in the truck," *he said. Thanks, Jack.*

I bring some snow in a plastic container along with a white pine branch from the side yard. A bit of the smell of fresh air and winter. (I think the nurses enjoyed it more than Chris.) I bring lavender essential oil to sprinkle on his pillow. Chris was too out of it to engage, but again the nurses loved it.

More pitons: Chris is eating more food and drinking more water. Now, I'm encouraging Chris to: use the breathing apparatus; drink some water; change positions; eat lean protein and veggies. And just eat more.

My heart pangs, watching my big strong husband struggle to get one little blue ball to the top of the little plastic breathing toy. I hate that thing. I want to throw it across the room. I bring it to him every 2 to 3 hours and urge him to practice breathing instead.

When will the lung drainage tubes come out? They say that pain will reduce when they come out. When? Today? No. This afternoon? No. Tonight? No.

Another day. The same. He takes a full walk around the ICU nurse's station. Another round of calls to family. People are calling & texting & Facebooking. I'm okay with not being social these days.

People continue to ask, but I don't know what I need other than getting the drainage tubes out of Chris' body and get the pain meds right. I just focus on the next piton.

The foley catheter comes out. That's a good thing (except Chris would rather not get up to pee. He'd rather stay in bed and let it drain. Too tired and too painful to move.)

I want most people to go away and leave us alone. Wait. I can't stand just sitting here alone, watching him labor his breath and struggle with pain to shift position.

My heart says, "It's okay, Honey. I'll just sit and hold your hand. You can rest. I know it's hard to sleep. You can rest."

When will they take these drainage tubes out? They're so disgusting. And, just like that, a Physician's Assistant comes in to take the tubes out. He says I can watch. No WAY! Total ick. After they're removed, Chris falls asleep. A deep sleep. For real this time. So precious.

Okay, next step: when does he get out of ICU? Today! Friends come by the ICU at the very moment Chris is being moved to the new "cardiac step down" unit. I ask them not to stay long when we're in the elevator. I tell them this move is going to exhaust him. They stand in his new room; I tell them again that Chris will now need to sleep.

Again, wanting real rest for Chris. I sit in a chair by

*his side, holding his hand, scrolling through Facebook and text messages, struggling to catch up with all the questions and offers. I still don't know what *I* need. I still don't know.*

Ordering meals at the hospital feels cozy. This is not a good sign. Or maybe it is? Such improvement in so few days. I start singing the Doxology in my mind over and over. I sing it while driving home. I sing it while driving back to the hospital.

Praise God, from whom all blessings flow;

Praise Him, all creatures here below;

Praise Him above, ye heavenly host;

Praise Father, Son, and Holy Ghost. Amen.

The last pitons: Taking Chris' work clothes home and bringing in sweatpants, a razor and toiletry kit. The final one: they clipped the jumper cables from his chest. Rolled him downstairs in the wheelchair. The valet brought the car. I drove him home never before so carefully.

EPILOGUE

As Paul Kalanithi writes in When Breath Becomes Air *(My Book): "Given that all organisms die, what makes a virtuous and meaningful life?"*

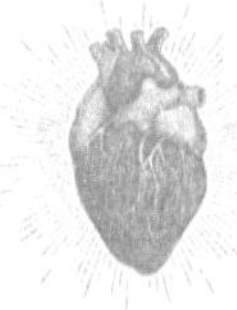

After about a month, I felt things were coming back into view (I'm editing this about three years after and thinking to myself, *That was nothing, boy. If you thought you were feeling better then, you're feeling at least much better now). Becoming clearer. More focused.*

Three weeks after surgery and feeling increasingly human.

Boy, I was out of it back then. My bowels were off track. They give you something that seems like it is named because someone thought it was a "Miracle Laxative." But I Googled that stuff and learned that it actually does something to the lining of your bowels. Yuck! No thanks. I took a couple of glasses of that stuff, and it seemed to take weeks for my system to get back on track. I credit Chobani (www. chobani.com) yogurt for most of the replenishing of the flora in my intestinal tract – important stuff to have inside you.

Okay, I'll have to do less straining everywhere. Whether that's in the bathroom, working in the yard, or carrying things and lifting things anywhere. No holding sneezes in. Less straining. Nothing over 50 pounds, the doc says. That's fine with me. I'm not sure I ever really seriously tried to lift anything over 50 pounds anyway. Less straining and 30 minutes of increased heart rate from exercise per day.

The "casual daily intimacy" that Rachel spoke of in the Love chapter, the intimacy she remembered the first time she crawled into my hospital bed, the intimacy we once nearly took for granted, isn't casual anymore. It no longer exists. Our intimacy is daily, but it's no longer casual. If it is anything, then it is intense.

We often cried in each other's arms with the weight of the moment, the weight of the Now present in our minds and in our hearts and that energy coming through our hands and our skin and when our lips embraced in a kiss.

It is a transference, a removal of external and internal boundaries and other obstacles to love and understanding so that the present and the future become momentarily boundless. The vastness of life reveals itself as limitless. There is an easing of the conveyance of love and the emotions that love carries and bestows on those lucky enough to experience it in its purest form. It cannot be faked or made up or constructed, and there are no strings attached. It is incalculable and immeasurable. It is infinite.

But from the casual intimacy, we had to the one we have now, a profound shift has taken place. A moving from the bedside chair into the hospital bed. A moving from laying beside one another and wrestling with wires and monitors to being with one another. A moving from the guest room bedroom to the master bedroom. A moving from teetering from the bedroom to the living room or kitchen, to climbing up the stairs again to the master bedroom. A non-negotiable transaction between loving hearts and knowing minds and laughing spirits that I can only wish were contagious. I can only wish it for others for it is infectious and it is a treasure to behold.

Rachel and I have been shown, and we have seen, that we are everything to one another and nothing without the other.

It is sometimes true, as Paul Kalanithi writes in *When Breath Becomes Air*, that we have to face losing everything to realize our full potential.

In talking about his experience as a priest and giving last rites, John O'Donohue wrote: "Usually people are so surprised that 'That was it,'" he said, which is particularly true of those who never lived the life they wanted or thought they deserved. Those who postponed life, allowed themselves to be contained by other people's expectations. Those who dreamed of a future that never came.

"Their life was squandered," he said.

But a deathbed, he said, is "the loveliest place to be if you're helping someone to die who has really lived."

Remembering one character, O'Donohue said he asked the man, "What would you say about the whole [life] thing now that you're about to leave it?"

A sly smile crossed the man's face. He told O'Donohue: "By Jesus, I knocked a hell of a squeeze out of it." Two minutes later, he was gone.

What are your fears? I continue to ask myself this.

The philosopher and poet John O'Donohue believed that we can transform our fear of death and, in doing so, we need to fear little else this life brings.

So, I ask, "What are you willing to sacrifice?" As humans, we live for something greater than and bigger than ourselves. If we can achieve it, does this make us successful in our life's mission?

Atul Gawande (My Book) writes that, more often than not, those who do achieve it, find death acceptable, or at least more so.

When it comes right down to it, he says, the questions you'll really care about are: What are your regrets, if any? Are you happy? Maybe: Did you achieve what you set out to achieve? Or were you successful in what you have done? Is there more you want to do? If so, then never stop pursuing that which you dream about. That's why it's there!

Today I more seriously consider living a life with meaning and leaving a legacy. Maybe it's this book.

This account of my thoughts about emergency heart surgery. Laughter, Love, Abundance, Understanding, Gratitude, and Hope. Maybe it's my friend who had aortic surgery because of what I went through. Perhaps I saved a life.

FACT: Most people's deaths come as a surprise.

FACT: There are two things that you can't fix: Aging and Dying.

As Gawande and others point out, one of the most difficult things to do is accept that life can be shorter than we'd like. What matters to most people is how their stories come to a close.

I hope that this has left you inspired, moved, relieved, renewed, or at least with something to think about.

Blessings.

http://llaughbook.com/

Christopher Zurcher is working as a housing coordinator with the Center for Disability Rights, a Connecticut Center for Independent Living. He received his Bachelor of Arts degree in English from the University of South Florida. He returned to Hartford in 1999 after 15 years in Central Florida, where he moved following a serious bicycle accident while riding cross-country for disarmament in 1982. Chris was a journalist for 15 years. He has blogged for the environment and peace and he enjoys creative writing, guitar and photography.

Rachel Heerema is an herbalist and master gardener and spends time thinking about growth, the seasons of the year, and the call of our souls to integrate back into a life rooted in our bodies and in nature. Rachel's background is nonprofit human sector work. She has a Master's degree in Business Administration and credentials as a Certified Professional Coach and a Reiki Master.

Pinwheels for Peace happened on the New Haven Green the year Chris and Rachel met – 2011 – with some help from the City of New Haven Peace Commission, New Haven Public Schools, and many others. The people behind the scenes have all changed with new school and city administrators in place. It is something Chris thinks should take place on every town green across the country on Sept. 21 – the International Day of Peace. Students make pinwheels and write and draw messages of peace on them and display them publicly for others to enjoy and learn from.